Off to Africa

Written by Sandy Roydhouse
Illustrated by Margaret Power

West Africa

Contents

Who Was Mary Kingsley?

Mary Kingsley was a British explorer who traveled to Africa in the 1890s. She explored rivers and forests that had never been seen by a European. She traveled by cargo ship from England to Africa, and then she traveled inland by canoe.

Few women traveled in the 1800s. Mary was very interested in learning about other people, and she was not afraid to travel to unmapped areas.

1862	1880s	1892	1893
Mary Kingsley is born in London, England.	Mary's brother is sent to Cambridge University. Mary and her parents move to Cambridge, too.	Mary's parents die within weeks of each other.	Mary makes her first journey to West Africa. She collects beetle and fish samples for the British Museum.

England in the 1800s

Victoria was the Queen of
England from 1837 to 1901.
This period in English history
is known as the Victorian Age.
Mary Kingsley lived during the
Victorian Age.

Africa in the 1800s

Many Europeans traveled to
Africa in the 1800s. However,
Africa is a very large continent,
and many parts were still
unexplored by Europeans
at this time.

Gabon Congo

AFRICA

Angola

1894	1897	Late 1890s	1900
Mary studies the local people on her second journey to West Africa. She also collects more samples.	Mary writes about her travels and publishes her experiences in articles and books.	Mary travels around England, giving lectures about life in West Africa.	Mary dies of a fever during an African war while volunteering as a nurse.

At Home in England

1870s–1880s

Sometimes Mary felt trapped. As a young girl living in Victorian times, she was expected to keep house and care for her parents and her younger brother, Charles. She longed to travel the world with her father, and she longed to go to school with Charles. Instead, Mary had to care for her bedridden mother. She hardly ever left the house.

bedridden   having to stay in bed because of illness

Mary Kingsley was born in 1862. Like many unmarried women of that time, Mary spent the first 30 years of her life at home, caring for her family and carrying out housekeeping duties.

Mary's father often spent nine or ten months each year traveling around the world. His letters home were filled with stories of his adventures in faraway lands. As a result, Mary developed a strong interest in travel.

Mary spent most of her childhood inside the grounds of this house at Highgate in London.

An Active Mind

Mary moved to Cambridge with her family so that Charles could attend the university there. Mary thought it was unfair that his university education was paid for, and that she was not allowed to go to college. Because she was so eager to learn, she read all the books in her father's library. Many of these books were about famous travelers.

Mary's father was very interested in studying people from earlier times. Through her reading and research, Mary was able to help her father with his work.
She was not allowed to travel with him, but she could find information for him about the places he visited and the people he met. He used her research and his experiences to write about his travels.

David Livingstone and Henry Stanley explored Africa in the 1800s.

Suddenly Alone

Mary had dreamed of freedom for a long time. However, when both her parents died within weeks of each other, she was filled with grief. She felt her life no longer had any purpose. She moved to a new house with Charles. But when Charles moved overseas, Mary knew the time had come for her to travel, too.

In 1892, at the age of 30, Mary suddenly found herself with no family to care for and no career. She was not used to being alone, and she became depressed.

However, Mary's research for her father had given her the idea of traveling to West Africa. When she decided to go there, some of her father's friends helped her pack a scientist's kit. Mary's aim was to collect samples of plants and wildlife to bring back to England.

When both her parents died suddenly in 1892, Mary was very sad. As was Victorian custom, she wore black clothing to show that she was in mourning.

depressed   feeling sad or gloomy

Off to Africa

Many people thought Mary was foolish to travel to West Africa. They warned her of wild animal attacks and deadly diseases. Mary was unafraid, however, and continued with her plans. She also ignored people who told her to pack men's clothing. She decided that her long skirt, long-sleeved shirt, and Victorian high-top shoes would be quite comfortable in Africa.

Mary traveled from England to West Africa on the cargo ship *S.S. Lagos*. Apart from a stewardess, she was the only woman on board.

The *S.S. Lagos* traveled down the coast of West Africa. On this trip, Mary traveled as far south as Luanda, in Angola. At various stops, she collected samples of beetles and fish to take back to the British Museum of Natural History.

Luanda, 1875

After traveling in West Africa for six months, Mary returned to London. She found life in London dull and dreary, and she wasted no time in organizing a second trip. By now, she was interested in meeting more African people, especially those who had never had any contact with Europeans. She wanted to discover more about how they lived. This time, Mary planned to explore inland areas of the large continent.

Mary went to Africa for the second time in December 1894. First she went to Nigeria, where African guides assisted her in paddling her canoe up the Niger River. She collected new fish samples from the mangrove swamps. However, the swamps were also home to many crocodiles, and on one occasion, Mary came very close to one bold, young crocodile, which climbed onto the front of her canoe.

Mary and her African guides paddled up the Niger River and then the Ogowé River.

The Ogowé River

Mary traveled by canoe up the Ogowé River, in Gabon. She was not disturbed by the heat, the wild animals, or the rough country. Mary loved Africa and all its sights and sounds.

Even though she was thrown out of the canoe and into the river many times, Mary thought the river was fascinating. She found new and interesting kinds of fish, and she loved the surrounding rainforest.

In Gabon, Mary's African guides took her into dense rainforest where no European had ever been before.

The Ogowé River was wild in parts, with whirlpools and large boulders blocking the way. None of this bothered Mary, however, and she continued to travel farther inland.

After watching a group of gorillas near the Ogowé River, Mary said, "*... never have I seen anything to equal gorillas going through the bush; it is a graceful, powerful, superbly perfect hand-trapeze performance.*"

Finding the Fang

Mary wanted to meet a tribe of people called the Fang. She found the first signs of them when she suddenly fell 15 feet into one of their animal traps. The pit was filled with sharp spikes. Luckily, Mary's thick layers of skirts and petticoats saved her from injury.

When Mary first came face to face with the Fang, they were hostile. Then, one of them recognized one of Mary's guides, and her group was welcomed and treated as guests.

hostile   unfriendly or angry

Mary spent about a week in Fang territory. She traveled from village to village, learning about the beliefs and customs of the Fang. She also acted as a doctor in each of the villages she visited. Although she found this journey very tiring, Mary enjoyed it. She grew to like the Fang people very much.

Mary enjoyed the company of the Fang. She found them intelligent and lively.

custom a special way of doing things

Speaking Out

Mary returned to England to write about her travels. Her first book, Travels in West Africa, *was published in 1897. Mary's thinking was quite different from that of many other people living in Victorian times. However, the tales of her travels helped her audiences have a better understanding of Africa and the people who lived there. Mary became a very popular public speaker. People were surprised that a woman had traveled alone to Africa and had such adventures.*

Although she had become a very successful writer and speaker, Mary longed to go back to Africa. When war broke out in South Africa in 1899, she traveled there to work as a nurse.

Mary worked in a prison where a fever epidemic was raging. She nursed many sick and dying prisoners. Sadly, Mary caught the fever from her patients.

Mary in Calabar, Nigeria, during her last trip to Africa. She is seated in the front row, center.

epidemic a widespread outbreak of an illness

21

A Brave Traveler

Mary Kingsley died on June 3, 1900, in South Africa. Although Mary's early life in England had been quiet and sheltered, her years of travel in Africa had shown that she was an adventurous and brave person. Her experiences brought her great happiness, and the books she wrote about her discoveries helped educate people about other cultures and countries around the world.

culture the ideas and beliefs of a group of people

Mary was buried at sea, according to her wishes. A British flag was draped over her coffin.

Promoting Understanding

By the late 1700s, Europeans had traveled to the coasts of Africa, but not many people had been inland.

In the late 1800s, Mary's travels took her far from home. Her work, and the work of other explorers during the 1800s, helped people around the world have a better understanding of the African continent at that time. Other explorers who traveled to Africa during this time include:

- David Livingstone (1841–1871)

- Richard Burton and John Speke (1857–1859)

- Samuel White Baker and his wife, Florence (1860s)

- Henry Stanley (1871–1877)

What If?

Mary did a lot of reading and research in her early years because she was "trapped" in her house. What if Mary had not spent most of her time at home? Do you think she would have developed such a great interest in seeing the world? Or do you think she would have been like many other Victorian women and never traveled outside her country?

Why do you think Mary Kingsley was so determined to travel to Africa, even though her friends warned her not to?

Index

determination a drive to succeed